Jackie Robinson

Stephanie Sammartino McPherson

LERNER PUBLICATIONS COMPANY • MINNEAPOLIS

To Dick

Illustrations by Tad Butler

Text copyright © 2010 by Stephanie Sammartino McPherson
Illustrations copyright © 2010 by Lerner Publishing Group, Inc.

Lerner Publications Company
A division of Lerner Publishing Group, Inc.
241 First Avenue North
Minneapolis, MN 55401 U.S.A.

Website address: www.lernerbooks.com

Library of Congress Cataloging-in-Publication Data

McPherson, Stephanie Sammartino.
    Jackie Robinson / by Stephanie Sammartino McPherson.
      p.   cm. — (History maker biographies)
    Includes bibliographical references and index.
    ISBN 978–0–7613–5207–5 (lib. bdg. : alk. paper)
    1. Robinson, Jackie, 1919–1972—Juvenile literature. 2. Baseball players—
    United States—Biography—Juvenile literature. 3. African American baseball
    players—Biography—Juvenile literature. I. Title.
    GV865.R6M43 2010
    796.357092—dc22 [B]   2009020585

Manufactured in the United States of America
1 – VI – 12/15/09

TABLE OF CONTENTS

INTRODUCTION

Jackie Robinson loved sports. Everyone could see he was a gifted athlete. When he was a young man, however, African Americans were not allowed to play professional baseball with white people.

Jackie changed that. He became the first African American baseball player on a major-league team in the twentieth century. As a Brooklyn Dodger, he endured insults and threats. He could not eat in the same restaurants or stay in the same hotels as his white teammates. Sometimes Jackie felt like quitting. But he stuck with the Dodgers and helped them become champions. He also fought tirelessly for civil rights. He showed that blacks and whites could live, work, and play together.

This is his story.

YOUNG ATHLETE

When Jackie Robinson was a baby, his mother took a big step. Mallie Robinson decided to start a new life for herself and her five children. Jackie wouldn't remember Cairo, Georgia, where he was born on January 31, 1919. He wouldn't remember his father, who had left the family on their own. And he wouldn't remember the long train ride across the United States to California.

Jackie's earliest memories were of Pasadena in sunny Southern California. That's where Mallie chose to raise her children. Jackie's mother worked hard cleaning the house of a white family. She saved her money. Then, in 1922, she and some of her relatives bought a house on Pepper Street in Pasadena. The house had five bedrooms, a big backyard, and a vegetable garden. The Robinsons called it the castle.

Jackie (SECOND FROM LEFT) stands for a picture with his brothers and sister. His mother, Mallie, is seated.

Jackie grew up in a white neighborhood. At school, he got his classmates' attention by playing sports. Jackie was so good that everyone wanted to be on his team. Sometimes children offered him extra food from their lunches if he would play on their side. Jackie liked these offers. There wasn't always enough food at home.

This photo of Pasadena, where the Robinsons lived, was taken in 1926.

When Jackie was young, many public swimming pools did not let African Americans swim with white people.

Jackie found it hard to be an African American in a white community. Some white neighbors had not welcomed his family. The YMCA, a community center, would not let Jackie join. And the local swimming pool was only open to African Americans one day a week.

Jackie's mother taught her children not to start trouble with white children. But she also taught them to stand up for their rights. Jackie developed a strong sense of justice. He hated the way African Americans were treated as second-class citizens.

Jackie and some Hispanic and Asian boys decided to form their own group. They called it the Pepper Street Gang. The boys got into lots of mischief. They threw balls of dirt at passing cars and stole fruit from orchards and stands. They grabbed stray balls off the golf course. Later, they sold them back to the golfers.

Several adults helped put Jackie back on the right track. Carl Anderson, a family friend, talked to Jackie about his mother. He told Jackie that his actions upset Mallie. Jackie listened carefully. He loved and respected his mother. He didn't want to hurt her.

SUPPORTIVE BROTHER

Jackie's older brother Matthew "Mack" was an athlete. He encouraged Jackie to participate in sports. In 1936, Mack competed in track and field at the Olympics in Berlin, Germany. He won a silver medal in the 200-meter race. Later, when Jackie set a college broad jump record, it was Mack's old record that he beat.

Jackie's brother Mack (FAR RIGHT) wins the 200-meter dash in the Olympic tryouts.

Jackie turned his energy to athletics. In high school and later at Pasadena Junior College, he starred in sports. In 1938, when he was nineteen, he set a national junior college record in the broad jump. His jump took him 25 feet 6½ inches. Moments after his triumph, he was off to a baseball game in a nearby town. Jackie helped win the game for Pasadena. That season, he led the team to the division championship.

That same year, the Chicago White Sox visited Pasadena for spring training. The Sox competed against some local young men. Jackie played a fantastic game. The Sox manager was impressed with him. But unfortunately, the manager shared the common prejudice of the times. "If that kid was white, I'd sign him right now," he said.

KARL DOWNS

In 1938, the Reverend Karl Downs became the pastor at the Robinsons' church in Pasadena. Twenty-five-year-old Karl Downs started clubs and teams for young people. He helped them see the importance of God in their lives. And he urged them to work toward equality. Jackie and his pastor became good friends. Jackie's family said his friendship with Reverend Downs "changed the course of his life."

2 MAKING A LIVING

After junior college, Jackie went on to the University of California at Los Angeles (UCLA). He continued to play sports brilliantly. An athlete who plays on the varsity (top-level) team in a college sport receives a large cloth letter to wear on his or her jacket. Jackie became the first person at UCLA to earn letters in four sports—football, basketball, track, and baseball.

Jackie practices with the UCLA football team.

In 1940, when Jackie was a senior, he met a freshman named Rachel Isum. He felt drawn to the pretty, studious woman with the warm smile. Rachel liked Jackie also. The two began spending time together.

But Jackie did not remain at UCLA long after he met Rachel. He decided that a college degree would not help an African American get a better job. Prejudice was too strong. Jackie dropped out before graduation in 1941. Rachel was disappointed. But the young couple continued to write and to see each other when they could.

Jackie took a job as an athletic director at a youth camp in California. When that ended, he went to play football in Hawaii with the Honolulu Bears. It was not a major-league team. But it did allow African Americans, and it paid a little. Jackie played football on Sundays. During the week, he worked with a building crew near Hawaii's Pearl Harbor.

When the football season was over, Jackie decided to return to California. He set sail on December 5, 1941. Two days later, passengers received word that the Japanese had bombed Pearl Harbor. Suddenly the United States was fighting in World War II (1939–1945).

Bombs explode in Pearl Harbor during the 1941 attack.

Almost four months later, Jackie was drafted into the army. After basic training at Fort Riley, Kansas, he applied to Officer Candidate School. But the school turned him down, along with other black soldiers.

Luckily, Joe Louis, a famous African American prizefighter, had also recently come to Fort Riley for basic training. He contacted important people he knew in Washington, D.C. Louis's complaints about the unfair treatment got results fast. The army admitted Jackie and others into Officer Candidate School.

Joe Louis argued that the army should let African Americans into Officer Candidate School.

Jackie wore his U.S. Army uniform for this photo in 1943.

Jackie became a second lieutenant in the army in January 1943. But he still faced prejudice. On a bus in Camp Hood, Texas, Jackie sat down with a light-skinned black woman. The bus driver may have thought she was white. At that time, blacks and whites could not sit together on buses. The driver ordered Jackie to the back of the bus. When Jackie refused, the driver called the military police. They accused Jackie of disorderly conduct. Jackie was put on trial. He was cleared of all charges, but he missed shipping overseas with the other men in his unit. Soon afterward, he decided to take an honorable discharge from the army.

Jackie had met a man in the army who had played for a black baseball team in Missouri. The Kansas City Monarchs played in a successful African American league. Jackie joined the team in 1945.

The pay, $400 a month, was great. But Jackie hated almost everything else. The team was constantly traveling. It was poorly managed. Many hotels would not let the players stay. They had a hard time finding good restaurants that would serve them. Jackie called this "a pretty miserable way to make a buck."

Jackie was twenty-six years old when he played for the Kansas City Monarchs.

Jackie did not know what to do. He wanted to make enough money to help his mother and to marry Rachel and support her. If he quit baseball, he might not be able to do those things.

In August 1945, the Monarchs were playing in Chicago. A man named Clyde Sukeforth introduced himself to Jackie. He told Jackie about a new baseball team for African Americans. It would be called the Brooklyn Brown Dodgers. Sukeforth said he was a scout for Branch Rickey, the president of the Dodgers. Rickey wanted to talk to Jackie.

After a few questions, Jackie agreed to meet Rickey in Brooklyn. Later, he reflected, "I figured I had nothing to lose."

3 "JACKIE STOLE THE SHOW"

Three days after meeting Sukeforth, on August 28, 1945, Jackie faced Branch Rickey in his Brooklyn office. Rickey got right to the point. There was no Brown Dodgers team. Rickey had wanted to keep the real reason for their meeting secret.

He believed the time had come to integrate baseball. That meant blacks and whites would play together on the same teams. How did Jackie feel about joining the Brooklyn Dodgers?

For an instant, Jackie was speechless. "I was thrilled, scared, and excited," he later recalled.

If Jackie and Rickey came to an agreement, Jackie would start out playing for the Royals. This was a minor-league team based in Montreal, Canada. Players got experience and sharpened their skills in the minor leagues. If they did well, they might be promoted to a major-league team.

This photo of Branch Rickey was taken in 1945.

But Rickey was looking for someone who was more than a great ballplayer. He was conducting an important social experiment. The first African American in the major leagues would face insults and racism. Rickey wanted a man who could control his temper. A player who responded angrily to racial attacks might set off a riot. That would make people less likely to support integrated baseball.

EARLY BASEBALL

Jackie was a twentieth-century pioneer. But about two dozen African Americans played organized baseball in the 1880s. Bud Fowler, considered the first black professional, played on various teams for fifteen years. In 1887, the International League, to which he belonged, stopped allowing blacks to play. By the early 1900s, organized baseball was basically an all-white game. The first all-black baseball league was formed in 1920.

"Mr. Rickey," asked Jackie, "are you looking for [an African American] who is afraid to fight back?"

"I'm looking for a ballplayer with guts enough not to fight back," replied Rickey.

Jackie decided he could be that ballplayer. He signed a contract to play baseball for the Montreal Royals. Soon he took another big step. In February 1946, he married Rachel in a large church in Los Angeles.

Jackie signs a contract to play with the Montreal Royals.

Jackie and Rachel hold hands shortly after they were married.

Several weeks later, the couple set off for Daytona Beach, Florida. Jackie was due to begin spring training there. The trip turned into a nightmare. After their plane landed in New Orleans, Jackie and Rachel were bumped from their next flight. Later, they were bumped from another flight in Pensacola, Florida. The Robinsons knew they had been denied places because of their race. Finally, they had to take a bus to Daytona Beach. As the seats began to fill up with whites, the driver ordered Jackie and Rachel to the back of the bus.

Things did not get better in Daytona Beach. The hotel where the other players stayed would not accept African Americans. Some of the cities where the Royals were scheduled to play practice games would not allow blacks and whites to play on the same ball field. Teams from three cities canceled games. In Sanford, Jackie had just scored a run when the sheriff arrived, dangling handcuffs. He said that the game was over unless Jackie stopped playing. Jackie remembered his promise to Rickey and sat down on the bench. But the sheriff was not satisfied. Blacks and whites could not sit on the same bench, he said.

Some people did not like to see Jackie (SECOND FROM RIGHT) sharing the field or the bench with his white teammates.

On April 18, 1946, the Royals officially opened the baseball season. They played against the Jersey City Giants in New Jersey. Jackie's presence drew crowds of African Americans. It also drew a large number of reporters.

Jackie must have felt nervous. But he played very well. He scored four runs and stole two bases. The Royals beat the Giants 14–1. The twenty-five thousand people in Roosevelt Stadium cheered loudly. An African American newspaper summed up the excitement: "Jackie Stole the Show."

Jackie (RIGHT) crosses home plate after hitting a home run in New Jersey.

Two weeks later, the team returned to its home base in Montreal. Many Canadians welcomed Jackie and Rachel warmly. It was a surprise and a relief after the prejudice they had faced in the South. The neighbors were especially kind to Rachel, who was expecting a baby.

Jackie traveled with the team for months. The Royals won enough games to go to the Little World Series. They played the Louisville Colonels in Louisville, Kentucky. Racial prejudice was still very much alive. People in the stands booed Jackie and yelled insults. He was too angry and upset to play well.

Baseball fans cheered loudly for their team. But sometimes they also booed loudly to upset players.

The Little World Series ended with games at Delorimier Stadium. It was the home field of the Montreal Royals.

When the series ended in Montreal, it was a different story. Jackie's outstanding performance helped the Royals win the series. "Jackie, Jackie!" cried the fans as they rushed onto the field. They lifted him onto their shoulders and sang. When he tried to return home, they chased him down the street. One reporter wrote that it was the first time that whites had run after an African American "not because of hate but because of love."

Jackie had had an excellent year in the minor leagues. Soon he and Rachel had another reason to celebrate. In November, their son Jackie Jr. was born. Jackie was thrilled to be a dad. But he was anxious to know what was next for him. Had he played well enough to be promoted? Would he become a Brooklyn Dodger? All he could do was wait and hope.

Jackie and Rachel sit with their new son, Jackie Jr.

4 "THIS YEAR IS A TEST"

The 1947 baseball season was about to begin. And still Jackie hadn't been promoted to the big leagues. One day, the Royals were playing a practice game against the Dodgers in New York. As Jackie rounded the bases, a statement was being handed out to reporters.

The announcement was signed by Branch Rickey. "The Brooklyn Dodgers," it read, "today purchased the contract of Jackie Roosevelt Robinson from the Montreal Royals." After the game, the Royals' manager handed Jackie a Dodgers uniform with a large 42 on the back. Jackie had made it into the major leagues!

The Dodgers played their first game of the season on April 15. Although Jackie was disappointed in his playing, the Dodgers won 5–3. "I know that this year is a test," Jackie told a reporter later that evening. He was determined to pave the way for more African Americans in baseball.

A city official (THIRD FROM LEFT) and a former senator (SECOND FROM LEFT) congratulate Jackie on opening day.

Jackie (FRONT ROW, SECOND FROM RIGHT) poses with the 1947 Dodgers.

Many of Jackie's fellow Dodgers did not welcome him in the beginning. Some had even tried to stop his promotion into the major leagues. Jackie's courage and great playing quickly won them over.

Players on other teams weren't always welcoming either. When the Dodgers played the Philadelphia Phillies, the Phillies yelled racial insults at Jackie. Their manager even urged them on. Jackie came close to cracking. But he kept his anger to himself. In the eighth inning, Jackie scored the only run of the day. He won the game for the Dodgers!

During his rookie (first) year as a Dodger, Jackie received hate mail and threats. But he kept his end of the bargain with Rickey. He did not respond to insults. Sometimes opponents tried to injure Jackie. Pitchers threw balls aimed at his head. Players running the bases tried to slash his ankles with the sharp spikes on their shoes.

Whatever happened, Jackie controlled his temper and focused on his playing. He hit well. And he became famous for stealing bases. Fans loved the way he danced around the bases, teasing the pitcher and infielders.

Jackie slides to steal second base during a game against the New York Yankees.

On September 13, 1947, *Sporting News* honored Jackie as the Rookie of the Year. His great playing helped the Dodgers win the National League pennant. That meant the Dodgers would play in the World Series.

Although the Dodgers fought hard, the New York Yankees won the series. Jackie hated to lose. But he had much to celebrate. After the game, each of his teammates came up to shake his hand. They said he was a fine player. Later, Jackie recalled, "I had started the season as a lonely man. I ended it feeling like a member of a solid team."

GOOD FRIENDS

During one game, people in the stands shouted insults at Jackie's southern teammate, Pee Wee Reese. They jeered at him for playing with an African American. According to one version of this story, Pee Wee walked over to Jackie and put his arm around Jackie's shoulder. The racist critics were stunned. Pee Wee and Jackie became good friends.

5 CHAMPION OF CIVIL RIGHTS

By the start of Jackie's second season, major-league teams had signed on at least five more African American players. Jackie was thrilled. The experiment had worked. Jackie had proved that blacks and whites could get along both on and off the ball field.

During his years as a Dodger, Jackie's family grew. In January 1950, his daughter Sharon was born. Then in May 1952, Jackie raced straight from the ball field to the hospital. He arrived in time to welcome his new son, David.

Jackie loved to spend time with his three children. He and Rachel built a large house in the countryside in Stamford, Connecticut. The family held swimming parties in the summer. In the winter, they invited friends over to play hockey and go ice-skating on the nearby lake.

Jackie celebrates his birthday. From left to right are Sharon, Jackie holding David, Rachel, and Jackie Jr.

The Dodgers run onto the field after beating the Yankees in the 1955 World Series.

Like all athletes, Jackie experienced highs and lows on the field. In 1949, Jackie was given the award of Most Valuable Player in the National League. One of his greatest thrills came in 1955, when the Dodgers beat the New York Yankees to win the World Series. But Jackie was already in his mid-thirties by then. His best days as a ballplayer were behind him. In 1956, Jackie retired from baseball. But he did not slow down. He took a job as vice president of a coffee shop chain called Chock Full o'Nuts.

The new job allowed Jackie to focus more time on causes important to him. He cared passionately about freedom and civil rights. He helped raise money for the National Association for the Advancement of Colored People (NAACP). He became involved in politics. And he helped create the Freedom National Bank. It was owned and operated by African Americans in the black community of Harlem, New York. He also spoke his mind on all sorts of current issues in his own *New York Post* newspaper column.

Jackie helped with Jackie Jr.'s Little League baseball team after retiring from the Dodgers.

Jackie (RIGHT) meets with Martin Luther King Jr. (SECOND FROM RIGHT) and other leaders of the civil rights movement.

In 1963, Jackie took his family to the nation's capital. They joined Martin Luther King Jr.'s March on Washington for Jobs and Freedom. They listened to King speak about his dream of racial equality. Returning home, they were determined to make that dream come true.

There was so much Jackie wanted to do. But his health was worsening. Jackie suffered from diabetes, a disease that affects blood sugar. He also had two heart attacks. His vision was weakening, and his legs often hurt badly.

Then his life was shattered. In 1971, his son Jackie Jr. was killed in a car accident. The love and support of his family helped Jackie get through the worst period of his life.

In the midst of his grief, Jackie continued to work for civil rights. He also started a construction company to build houses for poor people. And he wrote a book about his entire baseball career, titled *I Never Had It Made.*

Jackie comforted Rachel after Jackie Jr.'s funeral. Jackie's daughter, Sharon, is on the left.

Many people believed Jackie did have it made because he was famous and successful. But Jackie said he did not have it made while so many African Americans lived in poverty and were denied their rights. He wanted all citizens to be able to vote and run for office. "Until that day," he wrote, "Jackie Robinson and no one else can say he has it made."

Jackie holds a sign at a demonstration asking companies to give more jobs to African Americans.

ANOTHER FIRST

Several years after his retirement, Jackie was elected to the Baseball Hall of Fame. "I've been riding on clouds since the election, and I don't think I'll come down," he said at the ceremony. Jackie was the first African American to be inducted into the hall. A speech written by Martin Luther King Jr. was read at Jackie's celebration dinner. It applauded Jackie's "rich legacy of confidence and hope."

On October 15, 1972, Jackie was honored at the second game of the World Series in Cincinnati. Twenty-five years had passed since Jackie began his career with the Dodgers. By this time, almost a quarter of all baseball players were black. Jackie threw the traditional first ball to start the game and made a few remarks. He said he would like to see African Americans coaching and managing baseball teams.

Jackie lived only nine days after that. On the morning of October 24, he collapsed in Rachel's arms. He died on his way to the hospital. Tributes poured in from all over the country.

Jackie had done much more than open up professional baseball to African Americans. He inspired Americans of all races to dream big and stand up for their rights. "Life is not a spectator sport," he once said. "If you're going to spend the whole time in the grandstand just watching what goes on, in my opinion you're wasting your life." Jackie Robinson never wasted a moment.

Civil rights leader the Reverend Jesse Jackson (THIRD FROM LEFT) spoke at Jackie's funeral.

TIMELINE

In the year . . .

1920 Jackie's mother moved her family to
      Southern California.

1939 Jackie enrolled at UCLA.

1942 he was drafted into the army.   Age 23

1944 he was honorably discharged.

1945 he joined the Kansas City Monarchs.
      he met Branch Rickey.

1946 he married Rachel Isum.
      he joined the Montreal Royals.
      his son Jackie Jr. was born.

1947 he played his first game as a Brooklyn   Age 28
      Dodger.
      he was named Rookie of the Year.

1949 he stole 37 bases and batted .342 for
      the season.
      he was named the National League's most
      valuable player.

1950 his daughter, Sharon, was born.

1952 his son David was born.

1955 the Dodgers won the World Series.

1956 he retired from baseball.   Age 37
      he became a vice president of Chock Full
      o' Nuts.

1962 he was inducted into the Baseball Hall
      of Fame.

1963 he held his first jazz concert to benefit
      civil rights.

1971 his son Jackie Jr. was killed.

1972 Jackie was honored at the second game of   Age 53
      the World Series.
      he died on October 24.

44

MUSICAL FEASTS

In 1963, thousands of African Americans were arrested for marching for civil rights with Martin Luther King Jr. in Birmingham, Alabama. Jackie and Rachel wanted to raise money to bail them out of jail. They decided to hold a jazz concert at their home. Five hundred people came to hear the performers. World-famous musician Duke Ellington even showed up with his band, surprising everyone.

Rachel later called the occasion a "musical feast." The Robinsons made $15,000 to send to Martin Luther King Jr.

The jazz concerts became an annual event. Since 1973, funds raised from the concert have gone to the Jackie Robinson Foundation. Rachel founded this organization after her husband's death. The foundation gives scholarships to African Americans and to other minority students. Through the years, the foundation and the jazz concerts have grown. Jackie Robinson's legacy lives on through them.

FURTHER READING

Coombs, Karen Mueller. *Jackie Robinson: Baseball's Civil Rights Legend*. New Jersey: Enslow Publishers, Inc., 1997. This well-written biography provides lively and thorough coverage of Robinson's life.

Editors of Time for Kids. *Time for Kids: Jackie Robinson: Strong Inside and Out*. New York: HarperCollins, 2005. This short biography features photos from the *Time-Life* archives and an interview with Jackie Robinson's daughter, Sharon.

Lord, Bette Bao. *In the Year of the Boar and Jackie Robinson*. New York: Harper Trophy, 1984. A Chinese girl, new to the United States in 1947, is thrilled to meet her hero, Jackie Robinson.

Robinson, Sharon. *Promises to Keep: How Jackie Robinson Changed America*. New York: Scholastic Press, 2004. Jackie Robinson's daughter tells the story of his baseball career and contributions to civil rights. Many photos enliven the text.

Winget, Mary. *Martin Luther King Jr.* Minneapolis: Lerner Publications Company, 2003. Learn how a young pastor became one of the most influential civil rights leaders in history.

WEBSITES

Interview with Rachel Robinson
http://www2.scholastic.com/browse/article.jsp?id=4808
In this interview, Rachel Robinson talks about Jackie Robinson as a husband and father and as a civil rights activist.

National Baseball Hall of Fame and Museum: Hall of Famer Detail
http://www.baseballhalloffame.org/hofers/detail
.jsp?playerId=121314
This page includes links to videos of interviews with Jackie Robinson and Rachel Robinson as well as a celebration of Jackie's ninetieth birthday.

The Official Site of Jackie Robinson
http://www.jackierobinson.com/about/bio.html
This site includes a short biography with links to Jackie's baseball statistics, achievements, quotes, awards, and more.

SELECT BIBLIOGRAPHY

Eig, Jonathan. *Opening Day: The Story of Jackie Robinson's First Season*. New York: Simon & Schuster, 2007.

Falkner, David. *Great Time Coming: The Life of Jackie Robinson from Baseball to Birmingham*. New York: Simon & Schuster, 1995.

Rampersad, Arnold. *Jackie Robinson: A Biography*. New York: Ballantine Books, 1997.

Robinson, Jackie. *I Never Had It Made: An Autobiography*. New York: Ecco Press, 1995. First published 1972 by Putnam.

Robinson, Rachel. *Jackie Robinson: An Intimate Portrait*. With Lee Daniels. New York: Harry N. Abrams, 1996.

Simon, Scott. *Jackie Robinson and the Integration of Baseball*. Hoboken, NJ: J. Wiley & Sons, 2002.

Wilson, John R. M. *Jackie Robinson and the American Dilemma*. New York: Longman Pearson, 2010.

INDEX

Acknowledgments

For photographs: The images in this book are used with the permission of: © New York Times Co./Hulton Archive/Getty Images, p. 4; © Hulton Archive/Getty Images, p. 7; © E.O. Hoppé/CORBIS, p. 8; AP Photo, pp. 9, 11, 14, 16, 18, 21, 26, 36, 38, 39, 41, 43, 45; National Archives, p. 15 (W&C 1135); © Murray Garrett/Hulton Archive/Getty Images, p. 17; © Bettmann/CORBIS, pp. 23, 27, 31, 33; AP Photo/Ed Widdis, p. 24; © Rogers Photo Archive/Getty Images, pp. 25, 37; The Gazette (Montreal) © 1955, p.28; © FPG/Hulton Archive/Getty Images, p. 29; © Sporting News/ZUMA Press, p. 32; AP Photo/Marty Lederhandler, p. 40. Front Cover: © Bettmann/CORBIS. Back Cover: AP Photo/USPS.

For quoted text: pp. 7, 12, 26, 31, John R. M. Wilson, *Jackie Robinson and the American Dilemma* (New York: Longman Pearson, 2010); pp. 18, 19, 21, 23, 34, 41, Jackie Robinson, *I Never Had It Made: An Autobiography* (New York: Ecco Press, 1995), first published 1972 by Putnam; pp. 12, 42, 45, Rachel Robinson, *Jackie Robinson: An Intimate Portrait,* with Lee Daniels (New York: Abrams, 1996); p. 28, David Falkner, *Great Time Coming: The Life of Jackie Robinson from Baseball to Birmingham* (New York: Simon & Schuster, 1995); p. 30, Scott Simon, *Jackie Robinson and the Integration of Baseball* (Hoboken, NJ: J. Wiley & Sons, 2002); p. 42, Jonathan Eig, *Opening Day: The Story of Jackie Robinson's First Season* (New York: Simon & Schuster, 2007); 43, The Official Site of Jackie Robinson, n.d., http://www.jackierobinson.com/about/quotes.html (accessed September 18, 2009).